100

WORDS

for

Foodies

THE **100** WORDS ® *From the Editors of the*

AMERICAN HERITAGE ®

DICTIONARIES

D0981556

THE 100 WORDS® is a registered trademark of
Houghton Mifflin Harcourt Publishing Company.

Visit our websites: www.ahdictionary.com
or www.hmhbooks.com

ISBN-13: 978-0-547-23968-2

LIBRARY OF CONGRESS CATALOGING-IN-PUBLICATION DATA

100 words for foodies / from the editors of the American heritage dictionaries.
    p. cm.
  ISBN 978-0-547-23968-2
  1. Cookery--Dictionaries. 2. Cookery--Terminology. 3. Cookery. I. Houghton Mifflin Harcourt Publishing Company. II. Title: One hundred words for foodies.
  TX349.A115 2009
  641.3003--dc22

                                                          2009024582

Text design by Anne Chalmers

MANUFACTURED IN THE UNITED STATES OF AMERICA

1 2 3 4 5 6 7 8 9 10 - EB - 15 14 13 12 11 10 09

Table of Contents

100 Words

for

Foodies

EDITORIAL STAFF OF THE
American Heritage® Dictionaries

MARGERY S. BERUBE, *Senior Vice President, Reference Publisher*

JOSEPH P. PICKETT, *Vice President, Executive Editor*

STEVEN R. KLEINEDLER, *Supervising Editor*

SUSAN I. SPITZ, *Senior Editor*

LOUISE E. ROBBINS, *Senior Editor*

PATRICK TAYLOR, *Senior Lexicographer*

CATHERINE T. PRATT, *Editor*

PETER CHIPMAN, *Associate Editor*

KATHERINE M. ISAACS, *Associate Editor*

*Special thanks to cookbook editor extraordinaire
Rux Martin for her invaluable comments and advice.*

Preface

Most Americans have a voracious appetite for new and different foods, and no area of English comes from such a wide array of languages as the words we use for the foods we eat. *100 Words for Foodies* offers a fine selection of these words for your delectation.

The words represent the whole gamut of food—from ingredients to preparation to the dish on the table. There are words for implements and vessels like *mezzaluna* and *tagine* alongside the names of techniques like *macerate* and *deglaze.* There are spices like *epazote* and *fenugreek,* sauces like *nuoc mam* and *rouille,* and dishes from almost every cuisine imaginable: *baba gannouj* (Middle Eastern), *gado gado* (Indonesian), *pierogi* (Polish), *sancocho* (Latin American and Caribbean), *yakitori* (Japanese), and *zabaglione* (Italian).

Every word is defined, has a pronunciation, and an etymology. A number of words have recipes written by successful cookbook authors, and other words have notes that explain their surprising backstories. For instance, the seeds we call *coriander* we use to make curry powder. The shoots we call *cilantro* we put in salads and add as a garnish. But did you know that they both come from the same plant?

Talking about food is almost as much fun as preparing and eating it. We hope *100 Words for Foodies* adds savor and spice to your dinnertime conversation as well as your menu.

—Joseph P. Pickett,
Executive Editor

Guide to the Entries

ENTRY WORDS The 100 words in this book are listed alphabetically. Each boldface entry word is followed by its pronunciation (see page ix for a pronunciation key) and part of speech. One or more definitions are given with the central and most commonly sought sense first.

ETYMOLOGIES (WORD HISTORIES) Etymologies appear in square brackets following the quotations. An etymology traces the history of a word as far back in time as can be determined with reasonable certainty. The stage most closely preceding Modern English is given first, with each earlier stage following in sequence. A language name, linguistic form (in italics), and brief definition of the form are given for each stage of the derivation presented. For reasons of space, the etymologies sometimes omit certain stages in the derivation of words with long and complex histories, whenever this omission does not significantly detract from a broad understanding of the word's history. To avoid redundancy, a language, form, or definition is not repeated if it is identical to the corresponding item in the immediately preceding stage. The word *from* is used to indicate origin of any kind: by inheritance, borrowing, abbreviation, the addition of affixes, or any other linguistic process. When an etymology splits a compound word into parts, a colon comes after the compound word, and the parts (along with their histories in parentheses) follow in sequence linked by plus signs (+). Occasionally, a form will be given that is not actually preserved in written documents, but that scholars are confident did exist—such a form will be marked by an asterisk (*).

Several words in this book come from different varieties of Chinese. In etymologies, words from the Mandarin variety of Chinese are transcribed in the standard Pinyin system, using diacritic marks to represent the tones of the words. Words from the Cantonese variety of Chinese are transcribed using the standard Jyutping system, using superscript numerals to represent the tones of the words.

Pronunciation Guide

Pronunciations appear in parentheses after boldface entry words. If a word has more than one pronunciation, the first pronunciation is usually more common than the other, but often they are equally common. Pronunciations are shown after inflections and related words where necessary.

Stress is the relative degree of emphasis that a word's syllables are spoken with. An unmarked syllable has the weakest stress in the word. The strongest, or primary, stress is indicated with a bold mark (ʹ). A lighter mark (ʹ) indicates a secondary level of stress. The stress mark follows the syllable it applies to. Words of one syllable have no stress mark because there is no other stress level that the syllable can be compared to.

The key on page ix shows the pronunciation symbols used in this book. To the right of the symbols are words that show how the symbols are pronounced. The letters whose sound corresponds to the symbols are shown in boldface.

The symbol (ə) is called *schwa*. It represents a vowel with the weakest level of stress in a word. The schwa sound varies slightly according to the vowel it represents or the sounds around it:

a·bun·dant (ə-bŭnʹdənt)   **mo·ment** (mōʹmənt)

civ·il (sĭvʹəl)   **grate·ful** (grātʹfəl)

PRONUNCIATION KEY

Symbol	Examples	Symbol	Examples
ă	pat	o͝o	took
ā	pay	o͝or	lure
âr	care	o͞o	boot
ä	father	ou	out
b	bib	p	pop
ch	church	r	roar
d	deed, milled	s	sauce
ĕ	pet	sh	ship, dish
ē	bee	t	tight, stopped
f	fife, phase, rough	th	thin
		th	this
g	gag	ŭ	cut
h	hat	ü	*German* über
hw	which	ûr	urge, term, firm, word, heard
ĭ	pit		
ī	pie, by		
îr	deer, pier	v	valve
j	judge	w	with
KH	*Scottish* loch	y	yes
k	kick, cat, pique	z	zebra, xylem
l	lid, needle	zh	vision, pleasure, garage
m	mum		
n	no, sudden	ə	about, item, edible, gallop, circus
ng	thing		
ŏ	pot		
ō	toe		
ô	caught, paw		
ôr	core	ər	butter
oi	noise		

Easy Aioli

MAKES ABOUT 2 ½ CUPS

2 large egg yolks
1 small garlic clove, minced
2 teaspoons fresh lemon juice
2¼ cups extra-virgin olive oil
Kosher salt and freshly ground black pepper (optional)

In a food processor or a blender, blend the egg yolks, garlic, and lemon juice. While the machine is running, slowly pour in the olive oil in a thin stream. As soon as the mixture has thickened, spoon it into a bowl and season with salt and pepper, if you like.

—from *Cooking from the Hip* by Cat Cora

1 aioli (ā-ō′lē, ī-ō′lē)

noun

A rich sauce of crushed garlic, egg yolks, lemon juice, and olive oil.

[Provençal: *ai*, garlic (from Latin *allium*) + *oli*, oil (from Latin *oleum*).]

2 amaranth (ăm′ə-rănth′)

noun

1. Any of various annuals of the genus *Amaranthus* having dense green or reddish clusters of tiny flowers and including several weeds, ornamentals, and food plants. Also called *pigweed*. **2.** The grainlike seeds of certain species of this genus, traditionally used as a food in various indigenous cultures of Latin America.

[New Latin *Amaranthus*, genus name, alteration of Latin *amarantus*, never-fading flower, the cockscomb flower (*Celosia cristata*), from Greek *amarantos*, unfading : *a-*, not; + *marainein*, to wither.]

3 arrabbiata (ə-räb′ē-ä′tə)

adjective

Being or served with a spicy sauce of tomatoes, garlic, and hot chile pepper: *penne arrabbiata.*

noun

A sauce of this sort.

[Short for Italian *all'arrabbiata* : *alla*, in the manner of (from *a*, to, in the manner of + *la*, the) + *arrabbiata*, fit of anger, rage (in reference to the hot chile pepper used in such dishes; from *arrabbiare*, become rabid, be enraged, from *rabbia*, rabies, rage, from Latin *rabiēs*, from *rabere*, to rave).]

WORD HISTORY: The word *arrabbiata* looks like it might have been coined in Italian in reference to a dish borrowed from an Arab culture, but this is not the case. It comes from the Italian expression *all'arrabbiata*, which means "highly seasoned with pepper or other strong spices." This expression is derived from the Italian word *rabbia*, which means both "rage" and also "rabies"—dishes prepared *arrabbiata* are "enraged" with chile peppers, so to speak. The Italian word *rabbia* comes from the Latin word *rabies*, "rage, rabies," which is also the source of the English veterinary term *rabies* and, by way of French, of the English word *rage*.

4 baba gannouj (bä′bə gə-nōozh′) or baba gannoush (bä′bə gə-nōosh′)

noun

A purée of roasted eggplant and tahini, flavored with garlic and lemon juice.

[Levantine colloquial Arabic *bābā ġannūj* : *bābā*, papa + *ġannūj*, flirtatious (from *ġanija*, to flirt).]

5 bacalao (bä′kə-lou′) or bacalhau (bäk′kəl-you′)

noun

Codfish, usually dried and salted.

[Spanish *bacalao* and Portuguese *bacalhau*, both from Basque *bakailao*, probably from alteration of Old French *cabillau*, from Gascon *cabelh*, head (in reference to the cod's large head), from Latin *capitulum*, diminutive of *caput*, head.]

6 **bain-marie** (băn′mə-rē′)

noun

Plural: **bains-marie** (băn′mə-rē′)

A large pan containing hot water in which smaller pans may be set to cook food slowly or to keep food warm.

[French, from Medieval Latin *balneum Mariae*, bath of Maria, probably after *Maria Prophetissa*, an early alchemist who perhaps lived in Egypt between the first and third centuries AD.]

7 **beignet** (bĕn-yā′, bĕn′yā′)

noun

Southern Louisiana

1. A square doughnut with no hole: "*a New Orleans coffeehouse selling beignets, an insidious Louisianian cousin of the doughnut that exists to get powdered sugar on your face*" (Los Angeles Times). **2.** A fritter.

[French, fritter, diminutive of *beigne*, bump, lump, of Celtic origin; akin to Welsh *bôn*, stump.]

WORD HISTORY: New Orleans, Louisiana, has been a rich contributor of French loan words and local expressions to American English. Many New Orleans words, such as *beignet, café au lait, faubourg, lagniappe,* and *krewe,* reflect the New World French cuisine and culture characterizing this region. Other words reflect distinctive physical characteristics of the city: *banquette,* a raised sidewalk, and *camelback* and *shotgun,* distinctive architectural styles found among New Orleans houses.

8 | **bialy** (bē-ä′lē)

noun

Plural: **bialys**

A flat, round baked roll topped with onion flakes.

[Short for Yiddish *bialistoker kukhn*, cake or roll from Bi-ałystok, from *bialistoker*, of or relating to Białystok, from *Bialistok*, Białystok, a city in northeast Poland.]

9 | **biryani** also **biriani** (bĭ′rē-ä′nē)

noun

Plural: **biryanis** also **birianis**

A South Asian dish containing meat, fish, or vegetables and rice flavored with saffron or turmeric.

[Hindi and Urdu *biryānī*, from classical Persian *biryān*, roasted (equivalent to modern Farsi *beryun*), akin to *birištan*, to roast.]

10 blanch (blănch)

verb

1. To scald almonds, tomatoes, peaches, or similar foods in order to loosen the skin. **2.** To scald food briefly, as before freezing or as a preliminary stage in preparing a dish.

[Middle English *blaunchen*, to make white, from Old French *blanchir*, from *blanche*, feminine of *blanc*, white, of Germanic origin.]

11 bruschetta (broō-skĕt′ə, broō-shĕt′ə)

noun

Bread served in slices that have been broiled, rubbed with garlic, brushed with olive oil, seasoned with salt, and layered with any of various toppings such as chopped tomatoes, mozzarella cheese, or ham.

[Italian, from Roman dialectal Italian *brusco*, toasted, from *bruscare*, to toast.]

Slow-Roasted Tomato Bruschetta

MAKES ABOUT 45 HORS D'OEUVRES

4 pounds plum tomatoes (20–25), halved lengthwise
6 garlic cloves, minced
8 tablespoons extra-virgin olive oil
1 1/2 teaspoons salt
Freshly ground black pepper
1 (22- to 26-inch-long) baguette, cut into 40–50 (1/2-inch-thick) slices

Position racks in upper and lower thirds of oven and preheat oven to 200°F.

ROAST THE TOMATOES: Put tomatoes cut sides up on two large baking sheets with sides. Stir together garlic and 5 tablespoons oil and spoon over tomatoes. Sprinkle with 1 teaspoon salt and season with pepper. Roast, switching position of sheets halfway through roasting, for 6 hours; tomatoes will shrink but retain their shape. Let cool slightly. Increase oven temperature to 350°F.

MAKE THE TOASTS: Arrange bread in one layer on two large baking sheets with sides and brush with remaining 3 tablespoons oil. Sprinkle with remaining 1/2 teaspoon salt and season with pepper.

Bake, switching positions of sheets halfway through baking, until pale golden and crisp, 10 to 12 minutes.

Place a tomato half on each slice of toast and arrange bruschetta on two platters. Serve warm or at room temperature.

—from *The Gourmet Cookbook*, edited by Ruth Reichl

12 bulgogi (bo͞ol-gō′gē, po͞ol-gō′gē)

noun

A Korean dish made from sliced beef that has been marinated in soy sauce, sesame oil, garlic, sugar, and other ingredients and grilled, usually eaten by wrapping the meat and accompanying condiments with lettuce leaves into bite-sized morsels.

[Korean *bul*, fire + *gogi*, meat (so called because the dish was traditionally grilled over an open flame).]

13 cardamom (kär′də-məm) or cardamon (kär′də-mən)

noun

1a. An herb (*Elettaria cardamomum*) native to South Asia, having capsular fruits with aromatic seeds used as a spice or condiment. **b.** The seeds of this plant. **2.** Any of several plants of the related genus *Amomum*, used as a substitute for cardamom.

[Middle English *cardamome*, from Old French *cardemome*, from Latin *cardamōmum*, from Greek *kardamōmon* : *kardamon*, cress + *amōmon*, an Indian spice.]

14   ceviche or seviche   (sə-vē′chā)

noun

Raw fish marinated in lime or lemon juice with olive oil and spices and served as an appetizer.

[Spanish, from Arabic *sakbāj*, meat cooked in vinegar, from a Middle Persian word akin to classical Persian *sikbā* : *sik*, vinegar + -*bā*, gruel, soup.]

15   chaat   (chät)

noun

1. *used with a singular or plural verb* Small, often fried food preparations eaten as snacks in South Asian cuisine and traditionally sold by street vendors. **2.** One of these preparations.

[Hindu and Urdu *cāṭ*, a lick, taste, from *cāṭnā*, to lick, taste, from Prakrit *cāṭṭēi*, he licks, probably of imitative origin.]

16 | **challah** also **chalah** or **hallah**
(kʜä**ʹ**lə, hä**ʹ**lə)

noun

A loaf of yeast-leavened egg bread, usually braided, traditionally eaten by Jews on the Sabbath, holidays, and other ceremonial occasions.

[Hebrew *ḥallâ.*]

17 | **chayote** (chä-yō**ʹ**tā, chä-yō**ʹ**tĕ)

noun

1. A tropical American perennial vine (*Sechium edule*) having tuberous roots and cultivated for its green, pear-shaped fruit. **2.** The fruit of this plant, eaten as a vegetable. In both senses also called *christophine*; also called regionally *mirliton*.

[Spanish, from Nahuatl *chayohtli.*]

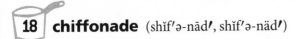

18 chiffonade (shĭf′ə-nād′, shĭf′ə-näd′)

noun

Herbs or vegetables cut into thin strips or shreds, often sprinkled onto a dish as a garnish.

[French, from *chiffonner*, to rumple, crumple, from *chiffon*, rag, scrap of cloth, from *chiffe*, old rag, alteration (perhaps influenced by Old French *chifre*, zero, thing of little value) of Old French *chipe*, from Middle English *chip*, wood shaving, chip, from Old English *cyp*, beam, from Latin *cippus*, post.]

19 chipotle (chə-pōt′lā)

noun

A ripe jalapeño pepper that has been dried and smoked for use in cooking.

[Mexican Spanish *chipotle* (also pronounced *chilpotle, chilpocle*), from Nahuatl **chīlpōctli* : *chīlli*, chile pepper + *pōctli*, smoke.]

20 choucroute (shoo-kroot′)

noun

An Alsatian dish of sauerkraut with wine, sausages, pork, and juniper berries.

[French *choucroute*, sauerkraut, alteration (influenced by *chou*, cabbage) of German dialectal *sûrkrût* : Old High German *sûr*, sour (akin to English *sour*) + Old High German *krût*, cabbage, kraut.]

Chipotle Chile Stuffed Eggs

MAKES 4 SERVINGS

$^1/_2$ teaspoon ground cumin

4 large eggs, hard-cooked, peeled and halved lengthwise

3 tablespoons sour cream or mayonnaise

1 tablespoon minced scallion greens

2 teaspoons fresh lime juice

1 canned chipotle chile in adobo sauce, finely chopped

1 teaspoon adobo sauce

$^1/_4$ teaspoon kosher salt

Coarsely chopped fresh cilantro for garnish

1. Place the cumin in a small dry skillet and toast over low heat until fragrant, about 10 seconds. Transfer to a small plate to cool.

2. Carefully remove the yolks from the whites. Place the whites cut side up on a plate. With the back of a spoon, press the yolks through a sieve into a small bowl, or mash them in the bowl with a fork. Add the sour cream or mayonnaise, scallion greens, lime juice, chipotle, adobo sauce and cumin. Mash with a fork until blended, then beat with a wooden spoon until the yolk mixture is smooth and fluffy. Add the salt.

3. Using a teaspoon, carefully stuff the whites with the yolk mixture, mounding the tops. Garnish each stuffed egg with a sprinkling of cilantro. Serve at room temperature or chilled.

—From *The Good Egg* by Marie Simmons

21 | cilantro (sĭ-lăn′trō, sĭ-län′trō)

noun

The stems and finely divided young leaves of the aromatic annual Eurasian herb *Coriandrum sativum*, used fresh in salads and various dishes as a flavoring and garnish. Also called *Chinese parsley, coriander.*

[Spanish *cilantro*, variant of *culantro*, coriander, from Late Latin *coliandrum*, from Latin *coriandrum*, from Greek *koriandron*.]

WORD HISTORY: The seeds of the coriander plant have long had a place in the various cooking styles of Europe. They are an important component in the spice mixes used to make many kinds of pickles and sausages. But the leaves of coriander have a flavor completely different from that of the seeds. By the end of the Middle Ages, coriander leaves were seldom—if ever—used in English cookery. There was no need for a separate English name for them like *cilantro*.

In the cuisine of many parts of Latin America, however, coriander leaves are an essential ingredient. The coriander plant is called *cilantro* in Spanish, and the Spanish word can refer both to the leaves and its seeds used as a spice. When Mexican and Caribbean food became popular throughout the United States in the middle of the 20th century, even Americans with no Latin American heritage acquired a taste for coriander leaves. When English-speaking foodies began to write down recipes for Latin American dishes containing the leaves, they tended to prefer *cilantro* as the name for the ingredient, rather than its English equivalent *coriander leaves*. Some people who had never grown coriander in their garden may not have even made the connection between the seeds in their jars of pickling spice and the leaves they bought at the Mexican bodega. Others may have thought that keeping a distinction between the meanings of *coriander* and *cilantro* was a useful way to avoid ambiguity. In a recipe for an Indian curry, for example, ground coriander seed will be added at the beginning, but the dish will be garnished with cilantro at the end. In this way, cilantro came to mean specifically "fresh coriander leaves" when used in English.

From the etymological point of view, coriander and cilantro are the same word. English coriander comes from the French word coriandre, and coriandre comes from the Latin word coriandrum. In medieval times, Latin coriandrum was sometimes pronounced and spelled coliandrum. (Perhaps people found it too hard to pronounce two r's close together in the same word, and one of them was changed to l). Coliandrum developed into the Spanish word culantro, and culantro also developed the variant spelling and pronunciation cilantro. This form of the word was then borrowed into English. The other form of the word, culantro, is still used in Latin America today as the name for an herb that is botanically unrelated to coriander but has a similar flavor.

The Latin word coriandrum itself is a borrowing of the Greek word koriandron, and the Greeks probably borrowed their word from an unknown language of the ancient Mediterranean region. Coriander was widely used in the ancient world—Tutankhamen's tomb contained a jar of coriander seeds intended to flavor the pharaoh's food in the afterlife.

22 couscous (ko͞os′ko͞os′)

noun

1. A pasta of North African origin made of crushed and steamed semolina. **2.** A North African dish consisting of this pasta steamed with a meat and vegetable stew.

[French, from Arabic *kuskus*, from *kaskasa*, to pulverize.]

23 croque-monsieur or croque monsieur (krōk′mə-syœ′)

noun

A buttery sandwich of ham, cheese, and sometimes béchamel sauce, that is often dipped in egg before it is grilled.

[French : *croquer*, to crunch, bite + *monsieur*, mister (from Old French : *mon*, my + *sieur*, lord, sir, from Latin *senior*, older).]

24 dahl or **dal** (däl)

noun

1. Lentils, peas, or other legumes that have been dried, hulled, and split. **2.** A thick South Asian stew made from such legumes with various seasonings.

[Hindi *dāl*, from Sanskrit *dalaḥ*, *dalam*, piece split off, from *dalati*, he splits; akin to English *tear*.]

25 deglaze (dē-glāz′)

verb

To dissolve the remaining bits of sautéed or roasted food in a pan or pot by adding a liquid and then heating the mixture in order to make a sauce: "*Add the wine, turn the heat back up to high, and deglaze the pan by bringing the wine to a boil and scraping the beef bits loose from the bottom of the pan*" (Eugenia Bone, *At Mesa's Edge*).

[*de-*, prefix indicating reversal or removal + *glaze* (from Middle English *glasen*, to glaze, from *glas*, glass, from Old English *glæs*).]

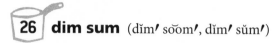

26 dim sum (dĭm′ so͞om′, dĭm′ sŭm′)

noun

A traditional Chinese cuisine in which small portions of a variety of foods, including an assortment of steamed or fried dumplings, are served in succession.

[Cantonese *dim² sam¹*, light refreshments : *dim²*, spot, drop (equivalent to Mandarin *diǎn*) + *sam¹*, heart (equivalent to Mandarin *xīn*).]

27 edamame (ĕd′ə-mä′mä)

plural noun

Fresh green soybeans, typically prepared by boiling in salted water.

[Japanese : *eda*, twig, branch + *mame*, bean.]

Edamame and Spinach with Golden Onions

SERVES 4 AS A MAIN COURSE

2 tablespoons canola oil

2 medium onions, halved and thinly sliced

2 medium garlic cloves, minced

2 pounds flat-leaf spinach, stems removed unless very thin, leaves washed, shaken dry to remove excess water, and chopped (about 12 cups)

12 ounces shelled frozen edamame (soybeans), about $2^{1}/_{2}$ cups

2 tablespoons soy sauce

Freshly ground black pepper

2 teaspoons toasted sesame oil

1. Heat the canola oil in a large casserole or Dutch oven over medium heat until shimmering. Add the onions and cook until golden brown, 8 to 10 minutes. Add the garlic and cook until fragrant, about 1 minute.

2. Stir in the spinach and cook just until it starts to wilt, about 1 minute. Add the frozen edamame, cover, and cook until the spinach is tender and the edamame are heated through, about 4 minutes.

3. Remove the cover and add the soy sauce and pepper to taste. Simmer to blend the flavors, about 2 minutes. Drizzle the sesame oil over the mixture and serve.

—from *A Year in a Vegetarian Kitchen* by Jack Bishop

28 emulsify (ĭ-mŭl′sə-fī′)

verb

To combine two liquids that normally will not mix together in such a way that one (such as oil) is dispersed as small droplets throughout the other (such as water).

[From *emulsion*, suspension of small globules of one liquid in another, from New Latin *ēmulsiō, ēmulsiōn-*, from Latin *ēmulsus*, past participle of *ēmulgēre*, to milk out : *ē-, ex-*, ex- + *mulgēre*, to milk; akin to English *milk*.]

29 epazote (ĕp′ə-zō′tĕ)

noun

The pungent leaves of the wormseed plant, used as a seasoning in Mexican cooking.

[American Spanish, from Nahuatl *epazōtl*.]

 **WORD HISTORY:** Epazote is a common ingredient in Mexican bean dishes—tradition has it that the herb makes beans easier to digest. When eaten raw, some people think that whole, fresh epazote leaves taste like machine oil, or worse, but when added to a large pot of beans, a small quantity of epazote imparts a distinctively earthy flavor that nothing else can replace. Many people have already known and loved epazote in good Mexican food without even knowing it.

The English name for this plant, *epazote*, is borrowed from Spanish, and the Spanish word itself comes from the Nahuatl word *epazotl*. Nahuatl was the language of the rulers of the Aztec Empire of Mexico that was conquered by Spain in 1521, and around a million and a half people in Mexico still speak Nahuatl dialects today, mostly in rural communities. Many other words for foods originating in the Americas have come into English from Nahuatl, after passing through Spanish along the way. This book, for example, includes five other words of Nahuatl origin: *chayote, chipotle, mole, nopal,* and *tamale.* Other words for familiar foodstuffs that come from Nahuatl are *cacao* (from Nahuatl *cacahuatl*) and *chile* (from Nahuatl *chīlli*). *Tomato* comes from Nahuatl *tomatl,* a word that usually refers to tart green tomatillos (large red tomatoes are specifically called *xītomatl* in Nahuatl). The English word *avocado* comes from Nahuatl *āhuacatl,* and *mole,* the word for savory Mexican sauces often flavored with chocolate, comes from Nahuatl *mōlli,* "sauce." When you put these last two Nahuatl words together, you get *āhuacamōlli,* literally "avocado sauce"—the source of the English word *guacamole.* Mesquite wood fires help give Tex-Mex food its distinctive tang, and the word *mesquite* itself is from Nahuatl *mizquitl.* Other English food words of Nahuatl origin include *achiote, cuitlacoche, jicama, pozole,* and *sapodilla.*

Even *chocolate* has a Nahuatl name—it comes from Nahuatl *chokolātl.* The chocolate eaten by the Aztecs and their neighbors the Mayans, however, was nothing like a modern chocolate bar. *Chokolātl* was a thick, unsweetened beverage typically made from ground cacao beans, corn flour, and the ground oily seeds of the kapok tree. These ingredients were mixed with water, spiced with chile peppers, and beaten into a froth with a stirring stick. Later on, Europeans took a sweeter approach to chocolate and prepared it with hot milk and sugar.

30 **falafel** or **felafel** (fə-lä′fəl)

noun

1. Ground spiced chickpeas shaped into balls and fried. **2.** A sandwich filled with such a mixture.

[Arabic *falāfil*, pl. of *filfil*, pepper, probably from Sanskrit *pippalī*.]

31 **farci** or **farcie** (fär-sē′)

adjective

Stuffed, especially with finely ground meat: *mushrooms farci.*

[French, past participle of *farcir*, to stuff, from Old French, from Latin *farcīre*.]

32 fenugreek (fĕn′yə-grēk′)

noun

1. A Eurasian plant (*Trigonella foenum-graecum*) in the pea family, having white flowers and trifoliate leaves. Its mildly bitter seeds and aromatic leaves are used as flavorings. **2.** The seeds or leaves of this plant.

[Middle English *fenigrek*, from Old French *fenegrec*, from Latin *faenum Graecum* : *faenum*, hay + *Graecum*, neuter of *Graecus*, Greek (from Greek *Graikos*, a member of the Graikoi, a Greek tribe that emigrated to Italy in the 8th century BC).]

33 Florentine (flôr′ən-tēn′, flôr′ən-tīn′)

adjective

Prepared, cooked, or served with spinach.

[Latin *Flōrentīnus*, of or from the city of Florence, Italy, from *Flōrentia*, Florence.]

34 focaccia (fō-kä′chə)

noun

A flat Italian bread traditionally flavored with olive oil and salt and often topped with herbs, onions, or other items.

[Italian *focaccia*, hearth-cake, from Late Latin, from *focācia*, feminine of *focācius*, of the hearth, from Latin *focus*, hearth.]

35 fufu or fu-fu (fōo′fōo′)

noun

A thick, doughlike West African food made by boiling and pounding a starchy vegetable such as yam, plantain, or cassava.

[Of West African origin; akin to Ewe *fufu*, Twi *fufuu*, and Yoruba *fùfú*.]

36 gado gado (gä′dō gä′dō)

noun

An Indonesian salad of mixed vegetables dressed with a peanut and coconut milk sauce.

[Indonesian, from *menggado*, to eat side dishes without rice.]

37 galangal (găl′ən-găl′, gə-lăng′gəl)

noun

1. Either of two plants (*Alpinia galanga* or *A. officinarum*) of eastern Asia, having pungent, aromatic rhizomes used medicinally and as seasoning. **2.** The dried rhizomes of either of these plants.

[Variant of earlier *galingale*, from Middle English *galingale*, a kind of root, from Old French *galingal*, from Arabic *ḥulunjān, ḥulunjān*, from Persian *ḥalanjān*, ultimately from a medieval Chinese word equivalent to modern Mandarin *Gāoliáng jiāng*, literally, ginger from Gaozhou : *Gāoliáng*, former name of Gaozhou, an area in Guangdong province + *jiāng*, ginger.]

38 | ganache (gə-näsh′)

noun

A rich icing made of chocolate and cream heated and stirred together, used also as a filling, as for cakes or pastry.

[French *ganache*, jowl, idiot, old fool, ganache (said to be so named because the icing was first prepared after a worker accidentally dropped chocolate into cream and was scolded with the word *ganache*).]

39 | garam masala (gä-räm′ mä-sä′lä)

noun

A blend of dry-roasted, ground spices, such as black pepper, cumin, cloves, and cardamom, used in South Asian cuisine to season meat, vegetables, or tea.

[Urdu *garm maṣāliḥ, garam masālā,* hot spices : *garm, garam,* hot, burning (from Persian *garm,* from Middle Persian, from Old Persian *garma-,* heat) + *maṣāliḥ, masālā,* ingredients, mixture of spices (from Persian *masāleh,* from Arabic *maṣāliḥ,* plural of *maṣlaha,* benefit, from *ṣalaḥa,* to be good).]

40 garlic (gär′lĭk)

noun

1. An onionlike plant (*Allium sativum*) of southern Europe having a bulb that breaks up into separable cloves with a strong distinctive odor and flavor. **2.** The bulb of this plant.

[Middle English, from Old English *gārlēac* : *gār*, spear + *lēac*, leek.]

WORD HISTORY: Hidden in the word *garlic* is a figurative reference to its appearance. Garlic comes from the Old English word *gārlēac*, a compound composed of *gār*, "spear," and *lēac*, "leek, plant of the genus *Allium*, onionlike plant," which is the ancestor of the modern word *leek*. The compound may have been suggested not by the pungent taste of garlic, but by the similarity in shape between a clove of garlic and a spearhead or by the shape of the leaves of the garlic plant. The word *gār* developed from the word meaning "spear-power" in the prehistoric ancestor of the Germanic language group. (The Germanic language group is the group of related languages that includes English as well as Dutch, German, Danish, Swedish, Norwegian, Faroese, Icelandic, and the extinct ancient language called Gothic.) Linguists think this ancient word for "spear" was pronounced **gaizas*, and descendants of **gaisaz* can also be found as the element *Ger-* in some English names that are ultimately of Germanic origin, such as *Gerald*, meaning "spear-power," or *Gerard*, meaning "spear-hardy."

41 **gazpacho** (gə-spä′chō)

noun

Plural: **gazpachos**

A chilled soup usually made with chopped tomatoes, cucumbers, onions, peppers, and herbs.

[Spanish, from Latin *gāzophylācium*, treasury, poor box in a church (the soup eventually being so called because it contains a variety of items), from Greek *gāzophulakion*, treasury : *gaza*, treasure (of Iranian origin; akin to modern Persian *ganj*, treasure) + *phulax, phulak-*, guard.]

White Gazpacho with Almonds, Grapes, and Cucumber

SERVES 4 TO 6

2 cups chopped peeled English (seedless hothouse) cucumber (about 1 large cucumber)

2 cups seedless green grapes

1¹/₂ cups salted Marcona almonds or other salted almonds

1 small garlic clove, peeled

¹/₂ shallot

1 tablespoon chopped fresh dill

1¹/₂ cups cold vegetable stock or low-sodium store-bought vegetable broth

¹/₂ cup good extra-virgin olive oil

1 tablespoon sherry vinegar

2 tablespoons sherry

Kosher salt and freshly ground pepper

OPTIONAL GARNISHES:

¹/₄ cup sliced seedless green grapes

2 tablespoons crushed salted Marcona almonds or other salted almonds

1 tablespoon chopped fresh dill

Put the cucumber, grapes, almonds, garlic, shallot, dill, and broth in a blender and puree until very smooth. With the motor running, drizzle in the olive oil in a thin stream until the mixture emulsifies. Stop the motor and taste the gazpacho; it should be smooth and creamy (if slightly grainy). If it's still a bit chunky, more like salsa than soup, puree it for another minute.

Add the vinegar and sherry and puree on high for 1 more minute. Season to taste with salt and pepper. Serve at room temperature or refrigerate until cold. (The gazpacho can be refrigerated in an airtight container for up to 2 days.)

Ladle the gazpacho into bowls and garnish with sliced grapes, crushed almonds, and/or dill, if desired.

—from *Cuisine à Latina* by Michelle Bernstein and Andrew Friedman

42 gravlax (gräv′läks)

noun

Raw, thinly sliced, cured salmon seasoned with dill and served usually as an appetizer.

[Swedish : *grava*, to bury (from the original process of curing it in the ground) + *lax*, salmon.]

43 gremolata (grĕm′ə-lä′tə)

noun

A mixture of chopped parsley, lemon rind, and garlic, used as a garnish for osso buco (veal shanks braised in white wine) and other dishes.

[Italian *gramolata, gremolata*, from *gramolare*, to break apart (hemp or other plants) in a scutch or brake, from *gramola*, scutch, brake for scutching, of unknown origin (*gremolata* perhaps being so called because the texture of the garnish resembles that of plant material that has been pro-cessed with a scutch or brake).]

44 | **haggis** (hăg′ĭs)

noun

A Scottish dish consisting of a mixture of the minced heart, lungs, and liver of a sheep or calf mixed with suet, onions, oatmeal, and seasonings and boiled in the stomach of the slaughtered animal.

[Middle English *hagese*; perhaps akin to *haggen*, to chop.]

45 hamantasch (hä′mən-täsh′)

noun

Plural: **hamantaschen** (hä′mən-tä′shən)

A triangular pastry with a filling such as poppy seeds or preserves, traditionally served in Jewish communities around Purim.

[Yiddish *homentash*, alteration (influenced by post-Biblical Hebrew *'oznê Hāmān*, hamentaschen, literally "Haman's ears") of German *Mohntasche*, poppy-seed pastry : *Mohn*, poppy seed + *Tasche*, pocket.]

WORD HISTORY: Hamentaschen are traditionally served around the Jewish holiday of Purim, which celebrates the deliverance of the Jews from a massacre in ancient times. The story of Purim, told in the biblical book of Esther, is set in the ancient Persian city of Susa, where an upright Jewish man named Mordecai was living. Mordecai adopts an orphan girl, Esther, who grows into a young woman of great beauty. When she enters the Persian king's harem, she immediately becomes his favorite, and Mordecai often waits in the vicinity of the palace to get news of Esther. However, when the king's minister, an arrogant man named Haman, passes in front of Mordecai, Mordecai refuses to bow to him. Haman begins to plot Mordecai's death, and he convinces the king to order a massacre of all the Jews in the kingdom.

To prevent the destruction of her people, Esther invites the king to attend banquets she prepares for him. Greatly pleased with Esther, the king offers to grant her whatever she wishes, and she asks him to stop the massacre. Haman, realizing that Esther now has the king's favor and that his own fate lies in her hands, falls to his knees to beg her for mercy. The king, however, thinks that Haman is trying to assault her, and he orders Haman's execution. The king sends orders to stop the massacre and decrees that the Jews can arm themselves against any who

---

disobey the new orders, try to kill the Jews, and take their property. The Jews then hold a feast to celebrate their triumph over Haman's plot, and the holiday of Purim commemorates this occasion with acts of charity, good cheer, and the little pastries called *homentashn* in Yiddish and *hamantaschen* in English.

In Yiddish, *homentashn* literally means "Haman's pockets." *Homen* is the Yiddish form of Hebrew *Hāmān*, the name of the enemy of the Jews, and *tashn* is the plural of *tash*, "pocket, bag." However, there is no clear reference to Haman's pockets in the book of Esther. Could the word refer to the sacks of silver taken from the Jews that Haman promised the king? Or to the covering over Haman's head when he was led away to be executed? In fact, there is an entirely different explanation for the word *homentashn*.

The first certain references to pastries like hamantaschen in Jewish literature go back to the 1700s, and the tradition may have originated much earlier—even before 1300. Originally, the cookies were given a Hebrew name, *'oznê Hāmān*, literally meaning "Haman's ears." (The exact reason for this name is not known. It is sometimes said that it refers to the practice of shaming defeated enemies in ancient times by cutting off their ears and noses.) The later Yiddish name *homentash* (plural *homentashn*) probably results from the influence of the term *'oznê Hāmān* on *Mohntasche*, the German word for any pocketlike cookie filled with sweetened poppy-seed paste. *Mohntaschen* are popular cookies in many German-speaking areas today as in the past, and the word *Mohntasche* is a compound made up of *Mohn*, "poppy seed, poppy plant," and *Tasche*, "pocket," the German equivalent of Yiddish *tash*. The Yiddish equivalent of German *Mohntaschen* would be *montashn*. Because *Mohntaschen* or *montashn* were eaten around Purim in Jewish communities and were also called *'oznê Hāmān*, "Haman's ears," *Homen* eventually replaced the similar-sounding *Mohn* in *Mohntaschen*. In this way, the Yiddish word *homentashn* came into being, and then colorful stories about the origin of the name of "Haman's pockets" could be told to children as they munched on their cookies around Purim.

46 **hominy** (hŏm′ə-nē)

noun

Whole or ground kernels of corn from which the hull and germ have been removed, as by boiling in a solution of water and lye.

[Short for Virginia Algonquian *uskatahomen*.]

47 **hoppin′ John** (hŏp′ĭn jŏn′)

noun

A stew of cowpeas and rice flavored with pork, ham, or bacon, said to bring good luck if eaten on New Year's Day.

[Origin unknown.]

Hoppin' John

SERVES 6

1 cup small dried beans such as cowpeas or black-eyes
5 to 6 cups water
1 dried hot pepper (optional)
1 smoked ham hock
1 medium onion, chopped (about ¾ cup)
1 cup long-grain white rice

Wash and sort the peas. Place them in a saucepan, add the water, and discard any peas that float. Gently boil the peas with the pepper, ham hock, and onion, uncovered, until tender but not mushy—about 1½ hours—or until 2 cups of liquid remain. Add the rice to the pot, cover, and simmer over low heat for about 20 minutes, never lifting the lid.

Remove from the heat and allow to steam, still covered, for another 10 minutes. Remove the cover, fluff with a fork, and serve immediately.

—from *Hoppin' John's Lowcountry Cooking* by
John Martin Taylor

48 induction cooking (ĭn-dŭk′shən kŏŏk′ĭng)

noun

A cooking method in which a magnetic field generated by an induction coil induces an electric current in a magnetizable vessel placed within the field, with the result that the vessel heats up, but the cooking surface does not. Induction cooking is more efficient than traditional electric cooking because it avoids the inefficiency of first heating a cooking surface, which then must heat the vessel, and so less heat is wasted. By altering the strength of the magnetic field, someone using induction cooking can make much quicker adjustments to the heat of the vessel than are allowed by traditional electric cooking, since the amount of energy flowing into the vessel changes immediately.

49 injera (ĭn-jîr′ə)

noun

A thin, round flatbread of Ethiopian origin prepared by fermenting a batter made from teff flour and cooking it on a griddle, traditionally eaten by placing servings of accompanying dishes on top of one flatbread and breaking off pieces of another to scoop up bite-sized morsels.

[Amharic *ənjära*, perhaps akin to *gaggärä*, to bake bread.]

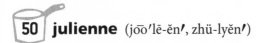

50 julienne (jo͞o′lē-ĕn′, zhü-lyĕn′)

noun

Consommé or broth garnished with long thin strips of vegetables.

adjective also **julienned**

Cut into long thin strips: *julienne potatoes; julienned pork.*

[French, probably from the name *Julienne*.]

51 junket (jŭng′kĭt)

noun

A dessert made from flavored milk and rennet.

[Middle English *jonket*, basket made from rushes, a kind of food served on rushes, feast, ultimately (probably via an Old French word akin to modern French dialectal *jonquette*, junket) from Latin *iuncus*, rush.]

WORD HISTORY: Junket is a traditional dish made by coagulating sweetened and spiced milk with rennet. In the United Kingdom, junket is considered a specialty of Devonshire, where it is often served with clotted cream (cream thickened by heating).

The rennet used to coagulate junket is a substance found in the stomach of calves and other unweaned mammals. It consists of enzymes that break down the proteins in milk and cause them to clump together in masses. Rennet is still used by traditional cheesemakers today to separate milk into curds and whey. The curds are then pressed and made into cheese. In medieval times, people obtained rennet by removing the inner membrane of the abomasum of calves and salting and drying it. (The abomasum, by the way, is the last or true stomach of the four organs called *stomachs* along the digestive tract of bovine animals. After other components of the hard-to-digest plant matter that cattle eat have been broken down and absorbed within the first three "stomachs," the food moves into the abomasum for the digestion of protein.) Pieces of this dried rennet were added to milk to prepare a variety of foods like cheese and junket and then removed once the milk had set. Later on, rennet became available in the form of an extract from calves' stomachs. Nowadays, a variety of products not derived from animals are available to coagulate milk, and these are called *rennet*, too.

In medieval times, soft cheeses and similar foods made from milk and cream were prepared in baskets woven from rushes or drained on layers of matted rushes. (Rushes are grasslike plants that often grow in marshy ground.) These baskets or mats would have allowed excess liquid to drain away while protecting the mass of coagulated milk or cream from breaking apart. In fact, the word *junket* originally meant "rush basket, especially one for carrying fish," and is ultimately derived from the Latin word *junca*, "rush." Since delicate dishes of cream or milk could be served in the rush baskets or on the mats used to prepare them, *junket* became the name for the dishes themselves.

The word *junket* then began to develop an interesting series of extended meanings. In the 1500s, it came to refer to an occasion at which a junket might be served—a banquet, feast, or bout of merrymaking in general. Then, during the 1800s in the United States, *junket* developed the meaning "picnic, pleasure excursion with eating and drinking." Americans began to use the word *junket* especially of trips taken by officials at public expense, ostensibly for fact-finding or diplomatic purposes but really just for the officials' own enjoyment. *Junket* also came to refer to trips taken by politicians or other influential persons as guests of a business or an organization seeking favors—a *junket* could be a bribe in the form of cruise tickets, basically.

52 | **kecap manis** also **ketjap manis**
(kĕch′əp mă′nĭs)

noun

A thick soy sauce of Indonesian origin that is sweetened with sugar.

[Indonesian *kecap manis* : *kecap*, savory sauce, soy sauce (probably from Xiamen Chinese *kôe-chiap*, fish sauce, akin to Cantonese *gwai¹ zap¹* : *gwai¹*, salmon + *zap¹*, juice, sauce) + *manis*, sweet.]

WORD HISTORY: *Kecap manis* literally means "sweet soy sauce" in Indonesian. *Kecap* is the word for soy sauce while *manis* means "sweet." It is no accident that the *kecap* in Indonesian sounds like English *ketchup*—they probably come from the same word in Chinese.

The ingredients used in the sauce called *ketchup* have varied over the years. The word *ketchup* first appeared in English in the late 1600s and originally referred to a sauce imported from China. This Chinese ketchup was quite different from the thick red tomato ketchup we now slather on french fries and hamburgers. Instead, its main ingredient was probably a liquid produced by fermenting fish or shrimp, like Vietnamese *nước mắm*. Eventually, Europeans and Americans began to make their own kinds of ketchup from more familiar ingredients like vinegar, anchovies, and mushrooms, and ketchup came to refer to something similar to today's Worcestershire sauce. Experimentation continued until, in the early 1800s, the first recipes for tomato-based ketchup begin to appear in cookbooks.

So as strange as it may sound, the word *ketchup* probably comes from a Chinese word meaning "fish sauce." In the variety of Chinese spoken in Xiamen, the word for fish sauce is *kôe-chiap*, a compound made up of *kôe*, "fish, salmon," and *chiap*, "juice, sauce." Xiamen was one of the main ports through which goods were exported from China to Britain, and there are many English words for Chinese trade items, like *tea*, that come from the Xiamen variety of Chinese.

It is very likely that this Chinese compound word meaning "fish sauce" is the source not only of English *ketchup*, but also of Indonesian *kecap*, meaning "savory sauce, soy sauce" in Indonesian. Since medieval times, Chinese merchants have traded actively in the seas south of China, and the Chinese word could have spread to the languages of the region easily. In fact, some language scholars believe that English *ketchup* passed through Malay, the language of Malaysia, before coming into English on its way from Chinese. Malay is very closely related to Indonesian—the two languages descend from the medieval form of Malay spoken around the Strait of Malacca between Sumatra and the Malay Peninsula. In Malay, the word for soy sauce has a slightly different sound from Indonesian *kecap* and is now spelled *kicap*. Ships carrying goods from China to India and Europe passed along these Malay-speaking coasts, so that European sailors often had the opportunity to pick Malay words like *kicap* and eventually bring them into English.

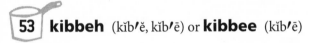

53 kibbeh (kĭb′ĕ, kĭb′ē) or kibbee (kĭb′ē)

noun

A mixture of ground beef or lamb, bulgur wheat, and spices, served baked, fried, or raw.

[From the colloquial Levantine Arabic pronunciation of standard Arabic *kubba*, ball, meatball.]

Turkish White Bean Wrap Sandwiches

2 15-ounce cans navy or other white beans, rinsed and
　　　drained
2 tablespoons minced fresh parsley leaves
2 medium scallions, thinly sliced
1 teaspoon Near East, or Aleppo, pepper
Salt
2 tablespoons fresh lemon juice
3 tablespoons extra-virgin olive oil
4 cups packed stemmed dandelion or other bitter greens
4 lavash wraps or flour tortillas (each about 12 inches in
　　　diameter), warmed one at a time in a large skillet

1. Toss the beans, parsley, scallions, Near East pepper,
and salt to taste in a medium bowl. Drizzle with 1 tablespoon of the lemon juice and 2 tablespoons of the oil
and toss again. Adjust the seasonings, adding salt and
Near East pepper to taste.

2. Toss the greens with the remaining 1 tablespoon
lemon juice and remaining 1 tablespoon oil in a medium bowl. Sprinkle with salt to taste and toss again.

3. Lay the warmed wraps flat on a work surface. Place
some greens on the bottom half of each wrap. Spoon
some beans over the greens and roll up the wraps, tuck-
ing the sides toward the center to form neat bundles.
Slice each roll in half and serve.

—from *A Year in a Vegetarian Kitchen* by Jack
　　Bishop

54 kimchi also kimchee (kĭm′chē)

noun

A Korean dish made of vegetables, such as cabbage or radishes, that are salted, seasoned, and stored in sealed containers to undergo lactic acid fermentation.

[Korean *kimch'i*, from Old Korean *timchoi* : Middle Chinese *trhim*, to soak, steep (source of Mandarin *shěn*)+ Middle Chinese *tshoj, tshaj*, vegetable, greens (source of Mandarin *cài*).]

55 lavash (lə-väsh′)

noun

A thin leavened flatbread of Armenian origin.

[From Armenian *lavaš*, Persian *lavāš*, and Turkish *lavaş*.]

56 linguiça (lĭng-gwē′sə)

noun

A highly seasoned Portuguese pork sausage flavored with garlic, onions, and pepper.

[Portuguese, from Old Portuguese *linguaínça*, from Vulgar Latin **longānicia*, a type of sausage, alteration (influenced by Latin *longus*, long, and possibly also *longāvō, longāvōn-*, a type of sausage) of Latin *lūcānica*, Lucanian-style smoked sausage, from *Lūcānia*, Lucania, an ancient region of southern Italy.]

57 lovage (lŭv′ĭj)

noun

Any of several plants in the parsley family, especially the Mediterranean species *Levisticum officinale*, having edible leaves and leafstalks and small, aromatic, seed-like fruit used as seasoning.

[Middle English, from Anglo-Norman *luvesche*, from Old English *lufestice*, from Medieval Latin *levistica*, from Late Latin *levisticum*, alteration of Latin *ligusticum*, from neuter of *Ligusticus, Ligurian*, from *Ligurēs*, the Ligurians, an ancient people inhabiting Liguria, a coastal region of northwest Italy.]

58 macerate (măs′ə-rāt′)

verb

To make or become soft by soaking or steeping in a liquid: *macerate shallots in vinegar; let grapes macerate in sugar and juice.*

[Latin *mācerāre, mācerāt-*, to macerate.]

59 madeleine (măd′ə-lĕn′)

noun

A small rich cake, baked in a shell-shaped mold.

[French, short for earlier *gâteau à la Madeleine*, cake à la Madeleine, perhaps after a cook by the name of Madeleine.]

WORD HISTORY: The little cakes called *madeleines* have been baked in France since at least the middle of the 1700s. They are considered to be the specialty of the town of Commercy in the Lorraine region of France. They were originally known in French as *gâteaux à la Madeleine*, "cakes à la Madeleine, cakes in Madeleine style," later shortened to just *madeleine.* This French name suggests that they were invented or made popular by a person named Madeleine. However, the identity of the Madeleine in question remains very much a matter of speculation. It is not even certain that she ever existed. The great French gourmand, Alexandre Balthazar Laurent Grimod de La Reynière (1758–1838), one of the originators of the modern notion of fine dining, attributes the invention of the madeleine to a certain Madeleine Paulmier, who worked as a cook for a certain Madame Perrotin de Barmond.

This Madeleine may or may not have been the Madeleine who appears in a popular and widespread story about the invention of the madeleine in Lorraine. The tale takes place at the court of Stanisław Leszczyński, exiled King of Poland and father-in-law of Louis XV of France. Stanisław, who also held the title of Duke of Lorraine, set up his court in exile at the château of Commercy in the 1730s. The details of the story vary from one telling to another, but they all attribute the invention of the cakes to a humble servant in Stanisław's employ named Madeleine. On one occasion, it is said, Stanisław's kitchen staff had failed to prepare a dessert for a banquet in honor of a great dignitary—or else the pastry cook had destroyed the dessert after a tiff with another member of the staff. Whatever the cause, disaster was averted when Madeleine whipped up a batch of little cakes according to her grandmother's recipe. Stanisław was delighted, and the cakes have supposedly borne her name ever since.

In the English-speaking world, the fame of madeleines was ensured by the French novelist Marcel Proust (1871–1922). Proust's masterpiece *À la recherche du temps perdu* (*In Search of Lost Time*) explores the relationship between life as it is lived in the present and life as it is transformed by memory. A crucial incident in the novel begins with a seemingly trivial action: the narrator tastes a bit of madeleine dipped in tea. On tasting it, however, a flood of vivid memories wells up within him, and the whole world of his childhood, the town where he ate madeleines with his aunt, springs to life in his mind. Proust's madeleine has become the symbol for this familiar experience, when a small detail—a bit of music, a whiff of perfume, the smell of a certain floor cleaner, the slant of sunlight in a room— transports us instantly back to our past.

60 | mandoline (măn′də-lĭn′, măn′dl-ĭn)

noun

A utensil consisting of a base into which adjustable blades are set, used to slice or cut fruits and vegetables.

[French *mandoline*, mandolin (musical instrument), mandoline, from Italian *mandolino*, diminutive of *mandola*, lute, ultimately from Late Latin *pandūra*, three-string lute, from Greek *pandoura*.]

61 | mezzaluna (mĕt′sə-lōō′nə)

noun

A curved steel blade, often with a vertical handle at each end, used to chop food.

[Italian, crescent, mezzaluna : *mezza* : feminine of *mezzo*, half (from Latin *medius*) + *luna*, moon (from Latin *lūna*).]

62 **mezze** or **meze** (mĕt′zā)

noun

1. Small, savory dishes served as appetizers or accompaniments to alcoholic drinks in Greek or Middle Eastern cuisine. **2.** A dish of this type.

[From Modern Greek *mezés* and Turkish *meze*, a mezze, and from Arabic *mazza*, appetizers, all ultimately from Persian *maze*, taste, relish.]

63 mole (mō′lā′)

noun

Any of various spicy sauces of Mexican origin, usually having a base of onion, chiles, nuts or seeds, and unsweetened chocolate and served with meat or poultry.

[American Spanish, from Nahuatl *mōlli*.]

64 mouthfeel (mouth′fēl′)

noun

The way that a food or drink feels in the mouth, being primarily a response to texture but also to flavor.

Chocolate Mole

MAKES ABOUT 4 CUPS

1/2 cup vegetable shortening
2 dried ancho chiles, stemmed and seeded
2 dried guajillo or cascabel chiles, stemmed and seeded
1 1-inch piece chile de árbol (or substitute 1 teaspoon
      cayenne pepper)
2 medium Spanish onions, coarsely chopped
6 6-inch white or yellow corn tortillas, torn into pieces
6 saltine crackers
1 teaspoon coriander seeds
1 cinnamon stick
1 star anise
1 whole clove
$1/2$ cup salted or unsalted roasted peanuts
$1/4$ cup sliced almonds
$3/4$ cup coarsely chopped bittersweet chocolate (about 6
      ounces)

Line a plate with paper towels. Heat the shortening in a small heavy skillet over medium heat. Add the chiles and fry, turning occasionally, until fragrant, 3 to 4 minutes. With tongs or a slotted spoon, transfer them to the paper-towel-lined plate to drain.

Add the onions to the pan and cook, stirring, until softened but not browned, about 4 minutes. Pour the onions and the shortening into a blender along with the chiles. Add the tortillas, saltines, coriander, cinnamon, star anise, clove, peanuts, and almonds and blend until a thick paste forms. Add the chocolate and blend until incorporated. Transfer to a bowl or other container. The mole can be refrigerated in an airtight container for up to 3 months; it does not need to be frozen.

—from *Cuisine à Latina* by Michelle Bernstein
and Andrew Friedman

65 | nacho (nä′chō′)

noun

Plural: **nachos**

A small, often triangular piece of tortilla topped with cheese or chile-pepper sauce and broiled.

[From *Nacho*, nickname of Ignacio Anaya, the maître d'hôtel of a restaurant in Piedras Negras, Mexico, who invented them in 1943.]

WORD HISTORY: A Tex-Mex favorite now eaten in every corner of the United States, nachos seem like a timeless dish—what could be simpler than melted cheese over tortilla chips? In fact, nachos are a comparatively recent invention, and they are named after Sr. Ignacio "Nacho" Anaya, who came up with the idea for them on the spur of the moment in 1943.

Sr. Anaya was the maître d'hôtel at the Victory Club restaurant in Piedras Negras, a city in the Mexican state of Coahuila located on the Rio Grande across from Eagle Pass, Texas. One evening a large group of guests arrived at the restaurant, and they needed something to nibble on. Sr. Anaya could not find the chef, so he went into the kitchen to prepare something himself. He took tostadas (corn tortillas deep-fat-fried until crisp), grated some cheese over them, and put them under the broiler. When the cheese had melted, he added some jalapeño pepper slices on top and emerged with the first plate of nachos ever made. His creation was a hit and came to be known locally as *Nacho's especiales* (that is, "Nacho's specials"). In Spanish, *Nacho* is a common nickname for men called Ignacio. Eventually *Nacho's especiales* was shortened to just *nachos*. The word *nachos* was then taken to be the plural of a common noun *nacho*, and now *nacho* is used in all sorts of phrases, like *nacho cheese flavor*.

Soon after their invention, nachos became quite popular in southern Texas, and somewhat later, in the 1970s, the well-known sports journalist Howard Cosell tasted them. He began to promote them at every opportunity, and the fame of nachos spread to every corner of the United States. To honor the creation of nachos, a nacho festival is now held annually in Piedras Negras.

66 nopal (nō-päl′, nō′pəl)

noun

Plural: **nopales** (nō-pä′lĕs)

1. Any of various cacti having edible stems, especially the prickly pears. **2.** The fleshy, oval, edible pad of such a cactus.

[American Spanish, from Nahuatl *nohpalli*.]

67 nuoc mam (nwôk′ mäm′)

noun

A pungent, salty liquid made from fermented anchovies or other fish, used as a seasoning and condiment in Southeast Asian cuisine. Also called *fish sauce.*

[Vietnamese *nước mắm*, fish sauce : *nước*, water + *mắm*, salted fish.]

68 orzo (ôr′zō)

noun

A pasta shaped like grains of rice, frequently used in soups.

[Italian, barley, orzo, from Latin *hordeum.*]

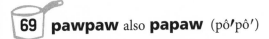

69 **pawpaw** also **papaw** (pô′pô′)

noun

1. Any of various deciduous trees and shrubs of the genus *Asimina* of the eastern and southeast United States, especially *A. triloba*, having purple flowers with three sepals and six petals and fleshy, yellowish-green, edible fruit. **2.** The fruit of any of these plants. **3.** A papaya.

[Ultimately from Spanish and obsolete Portuguese *papaya*, papaya, both from Cariban (language group of the Caribbean islands, Central America, and northern South America).]

70 **pho** (fō)

noun

A soup of Vietnamese origin typically consisting of rice noodles, onions, herbs, seasonings, and thinly sliced beef or chicken in a clear broth.

[Vietnamese *phở*, probably from French (*pot-au-*)*feu*, pot-au-feu.]

WORD HISTORY: The word *pho* is so identified with Vietnamese cuisine that many Vietnamese restaurants have the word *pho* in their name. In Vietnamese the word is written *phở* and pronounced with a tone that falls and then rises. But the word *phở* itself is probably not a native Vietnamese word. Instead, it is thought to come from French. Vietnam was a colony of France from 1885 to the beginning of World War II, and French influence is still felt in many areas of Vietnamese language and culture. It is likely that *phở* comes from the French word *feu*, "fire," in *pot-au-feu* (literally, "pot on the fire"), a stew of meat and vegetables cooked slowly over a low flame. It is also possible that the *feu* was originally the fire in the portable stoves carried by the traditional pho sellers walking down city streets selling their soup. These portable stoves were first introduced by the French. Whatever the route by which *feu* became *phở*, the word has been adopted into English as *pho* and is now on the lips of lovers of Vietnamese food throughout the English-speaking world.

71 piccata (pĭ-kä′tə)

adjective

Sliced, sautéed, and served in a sauce containing lemon, butter, and spices. Used of meat or fish.

[Italian, slice of meat cooked in butter, lemon, and parsley, feminine of *piccato*, larded, past participle of *piccarsi*, to prick oneself, translation of French *piqué*, past participle of *piquer*, to prick, lard.]

72 pierogi (pĭ-rō′gē)

noun

Plural: **pierogi** or **pierogies**

A semicircular dumpling with any of various fillings, such as finely chopped meat or vegetables, that is often sautéed after being boiled.

[Polish, dumplings, pl. of *pieróg*, pie, pasty, turnover, akin to Old Church Slavonic *pirŭ*, feast, from *piti*, to drink.]

 **73 polenta** (pō-lĕn′tə)

noun

A thick mush made of boiled cornmeal.

[Italian, from Latin, crushed grain, barley meal.]

74 ponzu (pŏn′zo͞o′)

noun

A Japanese sauce typically made from mirin (sweet rice wine), rice vinegar, bonito flakes, citrus juice, and sometimes soy sauce, often used as a condiment for seafood.

[Japanese, alteration (influenced by *-zu*, combining form of *su*, vinegar) of earlier *ponsu*, punch (containing citrus juice), ponzu, from Dutch *pons*, punch, from English *punch*, from Hindi *pañc-*, five, and related words in other South Asian languages (as in Hindi *pañcāmṛt*, Hindu ritual drink containing the five ingredients milk, yogurt, honey, ghee, and sugar, from Sanskrit *pañcāmṛtam* : *pañca*, five + *amṛtam*, nectar).]

Creamy Parmesan Polenta

SERVES 4

3 cups water

1/2 teaspoon salt

3/4 cup polenta (not quick-cooking) or yellow cornmeal (not stone-ground)

1 cup finely grated Parmigiano-Reggiano (about 2 ounces), or to taste

1 tablespoon unsalted butter

Salt and freshly ground black pepper

Bring water and salt to a boil in a 2-quart heavy non-stick saucepan. Add polenta in a thin stream, whisking constantly. Cook over moderate heat, whisking, for 2 minutes. Reduce heat to low, cover, and simmer, stirring for 1 minute after every 10 minutes of cooking, until very thick, about 45 minutes total.

Remove polenta from heat and stir in cheese, butter, and salt and pepper to taste. Serve immediately.

—from *The Gourmet Cookbook*, edited by Ruth Reichl

75 **poutine** (po͞o-tēn′)

noun

A dish of Québécois origin consisting of French fries topped with cheese curds and gravy.

[Québécois, probably of French dialectal origin (influenced by English *pudding*); perhaps akin to French dialectal (western France) *potine*, cast iron pot, or French dialectal (Normandy) *potin*, pâté.]

76 **purslane** (pûrs′lĭn, pûrs′lān′)

noun

A trailing plant (*Portulaca oleracea*) native to Eurasia, having small yellow flowers, reddish stems, and fleshy oval leaves that can be cooked as a vegetable or used in salads.

[Middle English, from Anglo-Norman *purcelane, alteration of Latin *portulāca, porcilāca,* purslane, from *portula,* diminutive of *porta,* gate (from the gatelike covering of the seed capsule).]

77 quahog also quahaug (kō′hôg′, kwô′hôg′, kwō′hôg′)

noun

An edible clam (*Mercenaria mercenaria*) of the Atlantic coast of North America, having a hard rounded shell. Also called *hard-shell clam, round clam*.

[Narragansett *poquaûhock*.]

WORD HISTORY: Quahogs and geoducks have nothing to do with mammals and birds in spite of the apparent similarity of their final elements—*hog* and *duck*—to the words *hog* and *duck*. Both *quahog* and *geoduck* were borrowed into English from Native American languages. The *quahog* is an edible clam that is found abundantly from the Gulf of St. Lawrence to the Gulf of Mexico. Its name is from Narragansett *poquaûhock*, "quahog." Narragansett, a member of the Algonquin language family, was spoken by a people inhabiting the area of Rhode Island. The Narragansett language is extinct, but some descendants of this group still live in Rhode Island today. *Geoduck* (improbably pronounced like *gooey-duck*) is the name of a big clam weighing up to twelve pounds and found in coastal waters from British Columbia to southern California and especially in Puget Sound. Its name comes from the Puget Salish word *gwídaq*, meaning "geoduck." Puget Salish is a member of the Salishan language family, which also includes other languages of the Pacific Northwest such as Bella Coola and Squamish.

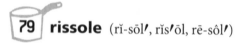

78 **ramekin** also **ramequin** (răm′ĭ-kĭn)

noun

1. A small ceramic bowl used for baking and serving.
2. A dish made with cheese, eggs, and bread crumbs or unsweetened puff pastry, baked and served in such a bowl.

[French *ramequin*, from obsolete Dutch dialectal (Bruges) *rammeken*, toasted bread, diminutive of *ram*, ram, battering ram.]

79 **rissole** (rĭ-sōl′, rĭs′ōl, rē-sōl′)

noun

A small, pastry-enclosed croquette of finely minced meat or fish, usually fried in deep fat.

[French, from Old French, from Vulgar Latin **russeola*, reddish paste, from Late Latin, feminine of *russeolus*, reddish, from Latin *russus*, red.]

80 rouille (rōō′ē)

noun

A creamy sauce of breadcrumbs, garlic, red chile peppers, olive oil, and often fish stock, traditionally served as an accompaniment to bouillabaisse.

[French, rust, rouille (in the latter sense, translation of Provençal *rouio*, rust, rouille, so called because of the sauce's reddish or tawny color), from Old French *rouille*, rust, from Vulgar Latin **rōbīcula*, from Latin *rūbigo, rōbīgo*, from *rōbus*, red.]

81 roux (ro͞o)

noun

Plural: **roux** (ro͞o)

A mixture of flour and fat cooked together and used as a thickening.

[French (*beurre*) *roux*, browned (butter), from Old French *rous*, reddish brown, from Latin *russus*, red.]

82 salsa (säl′sə)

noun

A spicy sauce of chopped, usually uncooked vegetables or fruit, especially tomatoes, onions, and chile peppers, used as a condiment.

[American Spanish, from Spanish, sauce, from Old Spanish, from Vulgar Latin *salsa, from Latin, feminine of *salsus*, past participle of *sallere*, to salt, from *sāl*, salt.]

WORD HISTORY: In English, the word *salsa* typically refers to a mixture of chopped tomatoes, onions, chile peppers, and other ingredients that accompanies Mexican and Tex-Mex cuisine. In Spanish, however, *salsa* is just the generic word meaning simply "sauce" or "dressing (as for a salad)." Each locality in Spain and Latin America has its own typical sauces. In fact, the Spanish word *salsa* and the English word *sauce* ultimately come from the same source.

The Spanish language evolved from the local variety of everyday Latin spoken in Spain during the days of the Roman Empire. The Spanish word *salsa* developed from the Latin word *salsa*, the feminine form of *salsus*, "salted." *Salsus* is the past participle of the Latin verb *sallere*, "to salt," derived from the Latin noun *sāl*, "salt." In this way, *salsa* is in origin just "a salted thing." Salt was of course an ingredient in most Roman sauces meant to accompany meats and vegetables, just as it is in modern sauces today. In the same way the local Latin of Roman Spain eventually evolved into the Spanish language, the local variety of Latin spoken in France in the days of the Roman Empire evolved into Old French, as the medieval form of the French language is called. Latin *salsa* developed into Old French *sauce*, and the Old French word was then borrowed into Middle English as *sauce*, the ancestor of the Modern English word.

The similarity in sound between English *salt* and Latin *salsa* is no accident, either. Modern English *salt* descends from the Old English word *sealt*, and the Old English word is closely related to the Latin word *sāl*.

Salsa is also a popular form of Latin American dance music, characterized by Afro-Caribbean rhythms, Cuban big-band dance melodies, and elements of jazz and rock. Many salsa aficionados have pointed out that salsa is an ideal name for "hot" music like salsa, and the name probably originates in cries like *¡Salsa!* given by Latin bandleaders when directing their musicians to "spice it up a little." The earliest and perhaps most famous use of such exclamations is found in the song *Échale salsita* ("Throw a little sauce on it!"), a classic from the 1930s by Ignacio Piñeiro, the great master of the genre of Cuban music called *son*, one of the ancestors of salsa. Ostensibly, the song describes a vendor of thick pork sausages called *butifarras*. During a night of revelry in the town, someone saunters past the vendor's establishment and hears him cry *¡Salsa! ¡Échale salsita!* as he deals out his sausage—Piñeiro's audience was of course free to interpret the sausage-seller's cry in other ways too.

83 | **sancocho** (sän-kō′chō)

noun

A stew or soup of Latin America and the Caribbean made from various meats, the tubers of the yam or the cassava (known in the West Indies as the yuca), and other ingredients.

[American Spanish, from Spanish, meat stew, from Vulgar Latin *subcoctus*, cooked a little : Latin *sub-*, under + *coctus*, past participle of *coquere*, to cook.]

84 | **shawarma** (shə-wär′mə) also **shwarma** (shwär′mə)

noun

Meat, especially beef, chicken, or lamb, that is roasted slowly on a spit and wrapped in pita bread, traditionally served with lettuce, tomato, and garlic sauce.

[Arabic *šāwirmā, šāwurmā*, from Turkish *çevirme*, a turning (in reference to the turning of the meat on the spit), verbal noun of *çevirmek*, to turn.]

WORD HISTORY: Shawarma is made by stacking thin slices of seasoned meat on a vertical spit, which is then slowly rotated near a fire. Pieces of the shawarma are shaved off the sides into a pan located beneath the spit in which the flavorful drippings of the roast are often allowed to collect. The meat is often wrapped in a pita with salad and condiments or served atop rice. Rather than being a dish prepared at home, shawarma is most often purchased from restaurants and fast-food stands that specialize in the dish.

The English spelling of the word *shawarma* is a fairly good representation of the sound of the Arabic word *šāwirmā* as it is pronounced in colloquial Arabic dialects—the everyday Arabic spoken by people as they work and eat in shawarma shops across the Arab world. Arabic *šāwirmā* itself comes from the Turkish word *çevirme*, literally meaning "a turn, a turning" and also "meat roasted by turning on a spit over a fire." *Çevirme* comes from the Turkish verb *çevirmek*, "to turn." In Turkey itself, however, the roasted-meat dish that is more or less equivalent to Arab shawarma is called by another name, *döner kebap*. *Döner kebap* literally means "turning kebab" in Turkish and comes from another word for "to turn" in Turkish, *dönmek*.

It is not surprising that shawarma, a dish so closely associated with the Arab world, should have a Turkish name. During the 1800s, the Ottoman Empire, with its capital at Istanbul, ruled much of the Middle East as well as a large part of eastern Europe. Turks, Arabs, Armenians, Greeks, Kurds, Slavs, Albanians, and many other peoples developed and shared common culinary traditions within the empire. These cultural interchanges continued in the eastern Mediterranean even after the demise of the Ottoman Empire in the early 20th century. The basic style of roasting meat called *šāwirmā* in Arabic and *döner kebap* in Turkish may have developed in the Turkish city of Bursa in the late 1800s and then spread to the rest of the eastern Mediterrean region and the Middle East.

It is also hard to miss the similarity between shawarma and the Greek style of roasting and serving meat that is called a *gyros* in Greek and a *gyros* or *gyro* in English. In fact, the Greek word *gyros* simply means "a turn," too. (The Greek word *gyros* is also the source of other English words relating to turning such as *gyre, gyrate,* and *gyroscope.*) *Gyros* was used to translate the Turkish expression *döner kebap* when shops serving this kind of sandwich began to be popular in Greece in the middle of the 20th century.

85 soba (sō′bə)

noun

A Japanese noodle made with buckwheat flour.

[Japanese, buckwheat, buckwheat noodle, short for earlier *sobamugi* : *soba*, edge + *mugi*, barley (in reference to the three-edged shape of the buckwheat seed).]

Soba Salad

SERVES 6

6 ounces soba (Japanese buckwheat noodles)

1 teaspoon Asian sesame oil

1 medium red bell pepper, cored, seeded, and cut lengthwise into thin strips

1/2 seedless cucumber (usually plastic wrapped), halved lengthwise, seeded, and cut into 1/8-inch-thick matchsticks

1/2 medium jicama, peeled and cut into 1/8-inch-thick matchsticks

2 ounces (2 cups) mizuna or chopped trimmed baby mustard greens

4 scallions, cut into very thin 3-inch-long strips

1 tablespoon seasoned rice vinegar

1/4 teaspoon salt

Bring 4 quarts water to a rolling boil in a 5- to 6-quart pot over moderately high heat. Stir in noodles and 1/2 cup cold water. When water returns to a boil, add another 1/2 cup cold water and bring to a boil again; repeat procedure once more. Test noodles for doneness: they should be just tender but still firm and chewy throughout. Drain noodles in a colander and rinse well under cold water, then drain thoroughly. Toss with sesame oil in a large bowl.

Toss together remaining ingredients in a medium bowl, add to noodles, and toss again to combine.

—from *The Gourmet Cookbook*, edited by Ruth Reichl

86 souvlaki (so͞ov-lä′kē)

noun

Plural: **souvlakia** or **souvlakis**

A Greek dish consisting of pieces of seasoned meat roasted on skewers.

[Modern Greek *souvláki*, skewer, souvlaki, diminutive of *soúvla*, skewer, from Medieval Greek, from Latin *sūbula*, *sūbla*, awl.]

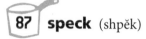

87 speck (shpĕk)

noun

A firm ham that is salted, spiced with juniper and other seasonings, smoked, and cured by drying, produced in the Tyrolean region of southern Austria and northeast Italy.

[Tyrolean German dialectal *speck* (akin to Modern Standard German *Speck*, bacon, blubber), from Middle High German *spec*, bacon, fat meat, from Old High German *spec*; akin to obsolete English *spick*, bacon, lard.]

88 tagine (tə-zhēn′, tə-jēn′)

noun

1. An earthenware pot used in the cooking of Morocco, consisting of a tall conical lid and a shallow base that doubles as a serving dish. **2.** A thick stew slowly simmered in such a pot, typically made of meat or poultry, vegetables, fresh or dried fruits, and spices.

[Arabic *ṭājin*, frying pan, shallow earthenware pot, from Greek *tagēnon*, *tēganon*, frying pan, of unknown origin.]

89 tamale (tə-mä′lē)

noun

A Mexican dish made of chopped meat and crushed peppers, highly seasoned, wrapped in cornhusks spread with cornmeal dough, and steamed.

[From American Spanish *tamales*, pl. of *tamal*, tamale, from Nahuatl *tamalli*.]

WORD HISTORY: Tamales are a daily staple in Mexico and many other parts of Latin America today, as they have been for thousands of years. The word *tamale* originates in Nahuatl, the language of the Aztec Empire that ruled central Mexico at the time of the arrival of the Spaniards in the Americas. The Nahuatl word for "tamale" is *tamalli*, and the Spanish borrowed this word as *tamal*. When English-speaking Americans who have learned a little Spanish travel south of the border, they are often surprised to learn this fact—that the Spanish word for a tamale is not *tamale*, but simply *tamal*. The plural of *tamal*, however, is the more familiar-looking *tamales*. *Tamales* is regularly formed according to the rule of Spanish plural formation: the plural of nouns ending in a consonant is formed by adding the ending *-es*.

As English speakers moved into new territory that the United States had acquired from Mexico after the Mexican-American War, they probably heard the plural *tamales* more often than the singular *tamal*. One average-sized tamale is often not enough for a meal, and so tamales are seldom eaten singly. (Who was ever satisfied by just one *raviolo*, instead of several *ravioli*?) In English, of course, the usual way of making plurals is just to add an *-s* to the singular of the noun. When circumstances forced English speakers to come up with a singular for the plural *tamales* , they simply performed this procedure in reverse and removed the *-s* to create the singular *tamale*, pronounced (tə-mä′lē). Linguists call this process *back-formation*. *Tamale* quickly became the more common singular form in English, despite the fact that the correct Spanish singular is *tamal*.

90 tatsoi (tät′soi′)

noun

An Asian plant (*Brassica rapa* subsp. *rosularis*) of the mustard family, having dark green, spoon-shaped, edible leaves that grow in a dense rosette. Also called *spoon mustard.*

[From Cantonese *taap³ coi³* : *taap³*, to collapse (perhaps in reference to its low, spreading rosette of leaves) + *coi³*, vegetable (or from an equivalent word in another variety of Chinese such as Mandarin *tàcài*).]

91 teff (těf)

noun

1. An annual grass (*Eragrostis tef*) native to northeast Africa, having very small, edible seeds and cultivated as a cereal crop and for livestock forage. **2.** The seeds of this plant, ground to produce flour.

[Amharic *ṭef*.]

92 tomalley (tə-mǎl′ē, tŏm′ăl′ē)

noun

The soft, green liver of cooked lobster.

[From a Carib language of the Caribbean region.]

93 umami (o͞o-mä′mē)

noun

A taste sensation produced by the presence of gluta-mates and nucleotides and associated with meats and other high-protein foods. It is sometimes considered to be a fifth basic taste along with the tastes sweet, sour, salty, and bitter.

[Japanese *umami* : *uma-*, stem of *umai*, tasty + *-mi*, noun-forming suffix (often interpreted in this word as Japanese *mi*, taste, from Middle Chinese and akin to Cantonese *mei*[6] and Mandarin *wèi*).]

WORD HISTORY: Many Japanese dishes begin with the preparation of a kind of stock called *dashi* (literally meaning "that which is made to come out" in Japanese). The simplest version of dashi is made from kombu (a kind of kelp) and flakes shaved off from dried filets of a tunalike fish called a bonito. These are boiled in water and then strained out from the result-ing stock (the bonito flakes often being wrung out in a cloth). The *dashi* can then be used as the base of soups, stews, and sauces. Miso soup, for example, is made from miso (fermented soybean paste) dissolved in *dashi*. *Dashi* can also be made from kombu alone.

The Japanese chemist Kikunae Ikeda (1864–1936) became interested in the chemistry behind the taste of kombu in *dashi*. In 1908, he discovered that the taste was due to the presence of chemical compounds called glutamates, such as monosodium glutamate. He gave the name *umami* to this flavor. *Umami* literally means "deliciousness" in Japanese. The word is formed from the adjective *umai* "delicious" and the suffix *-mi* that forms nouns from adjectives. (However, *-mi* can also mean "taste, flavor" in Japanese, so that many speakers of Japanese think *umami* is a compound of *umai* "delicious" and *mi* "taste" and literally means "delicious taste.")

Ikeda also thought he could taste umami in many other popular ingredients, such as tomatoes and meat stock, that are the basic building blocks of cuisines around the world. He found that these ingredients contained glutamates, too. Ikeda realized the commercial value of his discovery—"deliciousness" could be added to food instantly in the form of glutamates. He patented the production of monosodium glutamate in Japan, and it soon became a widely used flavor enhancer.

Later research has revealed that other compounds, namely ribonucleotides such as those released by cooking meat, also contribute to the perception of umami. Many cuisines of the word have a basic stock or sauce that includes one ingredient rich in glutamates and another rich in ribonucleotides, such as the kombu and fish flakes in Japanese *dashi*, or the tomatoes and drippings from browned meats in Italian red sauces. Foodies have benefited from our increased knowledge of the chemistry behind umami—chefs can now refine cooking processes to achieve the maximum release and beneficial combination of umami compounds.

94 | vindaloo (vĭn′də-loō)

noun

A highly seasoned dish of Indian origin made from meat or seafood cooked in a sauce of vinegar, red chiles, garlic, tamarind, and spices.

[From Konkani (Indic language of western India) *vindalu*, from Indo-Portuguese (Portuguese creole of Goa) *vin d'alho*, from Portuguese *vinha-d'alhos*, marinade or pickle for meat made from vinegar and garlic : *vinho*, wine (from Latin *vīnum*) + *de*, of (from Latin *dē*) + *alho*, garlic (from Latin *allium*).]

WORD HISTORY: The dish called *vindaloo* originated in Goa, a state of India on the coast of the Arabian Sea. The region that is the Indian state of Goa was once a Portuguese colony. The colony was established in the early 1500s, soon after Portuguese ships reached India and opened up the first direct trade routes from Europe to Asia. Goa prospered as a hub of Portuguese trade in Asia, although its importance began to wane in the 1700s. When the territories of India under British control gained their independence in 1947, Goa remained Portuguese. In 1961, however, an armed invasion of Goa by the Republic of India put an end to Portuguese control of the region, and Goa eventually became India's twenty-fifth state.

During the four and a half centuries of Portuguese rule in Goa, Portuguese traditions were incorporated into Goan culture, and many Portuguese words entered the local language of the region, Konkani. One Portugese culinary tradition that was successfully transplanted to Goa was *vinha-d'alhos*, a marinade for meat (especially rabbit and pork) made from vinegar, salt, lots of garlic, seasonings like bay leaves, pepper, and cloves, and often wine. Meat prepared with *vinha-d'alhos* is usually marinated in the mixture for around two days before being cooked and served. The name for this marinade, *vinha-d'alhos*, is derived from the Portuguese words for wine, *vinho*, and garlic, *alho*.

In Goa, *vinha-d'alhos* was transformed under the influence of local traditions. Garlic and vinegar remained prominent parts of the dish, but local flavors like ginger, cumin, and coriander entered the mix. Hot chile peppers were also added, and today, vindaloo has the reputation of being a fiery hot dish. (Although many cuisines of Asia now use large amounts of chile peppers in their dishes, chile peppers are native to the Americas and were first spread around the world along European colonial trade routes.) In Konkani, the dish was called *vindalu*, an adaptation of Portuguese *vinha-d'alhos*. In the United Kingdom and the rest of the English-speaking world, the dish eventually became well-known as *vindaloo*, a popular item on the take-out menu of Indian restaurants.

95 | **wasabi** (wə-sä′bē, wä′sə-bē)

noun

A very pungent green Japanese condiment made from the root of the herb *Wasabia japonica* of the mustard family.

[Japanese.]

96 | **waterzooi** (vä′tər-zoi′)

noun

A thick stew of Belgian origin consisting of fish or chicken, vegetables, broth, and seasonings, to which egg yolks and cream are added.

[Dutch : *water*, water + *zooi*, variant of *zoo*, boiled food, cooked food (from Middle Dutch *sode*; akin to Dutch *zieden*, to boil, and English *seethe*).]

97 xanthan gum (zăn′thən gŭm)

noun

A natural gum of high molecular weight produced by culture fermentation of glucose and used as a stabilizer in commercial food preparation.

[From New Latin *Xanthomonas* (*campestris*), name of the bacterium used to produce it : Greek *xanthos*, yellow (from the color of colonies of the bacteria) + New Latin *monas*, single-celled organism (from Late Latin, unit, unity, from Greek, from *monos*, single).]

98 yakitori (yä′kĭ-tôr′ē)

noun

A dish of bite-sized marinated chicken pieces grilled on skewers.

[Japanese : *yaki*, roasting, stem form of *yaku*, to roast + *tori*, bird.]

99 yuca (yōō′kə)

noun

The tuberous, starchy root of the tropical American plant *Manihot esculenta*, widely eaten as a staple food in the tropics after leaching and drying to remove cyanide. Also called *cassava, manioc.*

[American Spanish, from Taíno (Arawakan language of the Antilles).]

WORD HISTORY: Throughout tropical Asia, Africa, and North and South America, yuca, also called *cassava* and *manioc,* is one of the most important food crops, for it grows well in poor soils and its tubers are a concentrated source of carbohydrates. The yuca plant, whose scientific name is *Manihot esculenta* (meaning "the edible manioc" in Latin) is a somewhat gangly looking shrub or small tree with large palmate leaves. Although the plant probably originated in south-central Brazil and Paraguay, it has been cultivated in other tropical regions of the Americas for thousands of years.

Yuca was a staple crop of the Taíno, the indigenous people of Cuba, Hispaniola, and other Antillean islands who met Christopher Columbus on his first visit to the Americas in 1492. Since the Taíno introduced the Spanish to many foodstuffs native to the Americas, the Spanish words for these things come from the Taíno language. These words then spread from Spanish to the other languages of Europe like English. *Yuca,* for example, comes from the Taíno word for the yuca plant itself. *Cassava,* another English word for yuca, comes from the Taíno word *casabe* or *casabi,* the name of the breadlike food they prepared from yuca tubers. *Manioc,* yet another term for yuca, ultimately comes from Tupí. Tupí was the language of the indigenous people who lived along the coast of what is now Brazil, the homeland of yuca, when explorers and colonists began to arrive in the region from Portugal.

All parts of the yuca plant contain chemicals that are transformed into cyanide when that part is cut or otherwise damaged. In order to be made edible, yuca must be processed to remove the cyanide. Varieties of yuca producing tubers with low levels of cyanide are called *sweet,* while those with higher levels are called *bitter.* For sweet varieties, boiling or frying is enough to remove the cyanide, which dissipates harmlessly in the form of hydrogen cyanide gas. The bitter variety is often grated in large quantities, and then the gratings are pressed or wrung out in cloth in several changes of water. This washes out most of the cyanide while leaving the nutritious starch granules. The starchy mush is then often fermented, and the fermented product is used as a basic foodstuff in many cuisines around the world. The starch granules are also dried as a kind of meal, called *tapioca*—the tapioca used to make tapioca pudding. The word *tapioca* comes from Tupí *typióca,* a compound formed from Tupí *ty,* "juice," *pyá,* "heart," and *oca,* "to remove"—tapioca being starch grains squeezed from the inside of the tuber. The leaves of the yuca plant can be eaten, too, after being chopped, washed to remove the cyanide, and cooked.

The yuca plant should not be confused with the unrelated plants called *yucca* that have long, swordlike leaves and are often planted as ornamentals. Although the flowers and fruits of some yucca species are edible, yucca is not an important food crop. The similarity between the names of the plants is due to the Swedish botanist Carolus Linnaeus (1707–1778), who gave many plants and animals their modern scientific names. The common name *yucca* comes from *Yucca,* the name that Linnaeus created for the genus of the plants when he first classified them scientifically. Although Linnaeus probably based this genus name on Spanish *yuca,* the name for the tuber crop, we do not know exactly what reason he might have had for doing so.

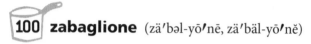

100 zabaglione (zä′bəl-yō′nē, zä′bäl-yō′nĕ)

noun

A dessert or sauce consisting of egg yolks, sugar, and wine or liqueur beaten until thick and served hot or cold. Also called *sabayon*.

[Italian, variant of *zabaione*, ultimately from Illyrian (language of Illyria, ancient region of the Balkan peninsula on the coast of the Adriatic Sea) *sabaium*, beer.]

Zabaglione

MAKES 4 SERVINGS

4 large egg yolks
1/4 cup superfine sugar
1/4 cup sweet Marsala wine

1. Place the egg yolks in the top of a double boiler or in a heatproof bowl that will fit snugly over a larger pan. Place on a folded kitchen towel and beat with a whisk or a hand-held electric mixer until pale yellow. Beat in the sugar about ½ tablespoon at a time, beating well after each addition. Beat in the wine.

2. Pour about 1 inch of water in the bottom part of the double boiler and heat to simmering, not boiling. Reduce the heat to low. Set the top of the double boiler or the heatproof bowl over the simmering water and beat the zabaglione with a wire whisk until thick and foamy, at least 7 minutes. Pour into 4 wineglasses or dessert bowls. Serve at once.

—from *The Good Egg* by Marie Simmons

Credits

The 100 Words

aioli
amaranth
arrabbiata
baba gannouj
bacalao
bain-marie
beignet
bialy
biryani
blanch
bruschetta
bulgogi
cardamom
ceviche
chaat
challah
chayote
chiffonade
chipotle
choucroute
cilantro
couscous
croque-
  monsieur
dahl
deglaze
dim sum
edamame
emulsify
epazote
falafel
farci
fenugreek
Florentine

focaccia
fufu
gado gado
galangal
ganache
garam masala
garlic
gazpacho
gravlax
gremolata
haggis
hamantasch
hominy
hoppin' John
induction
  cooking
injera
julienne
junket
kecap manis
kibbeh
kimchi
lavash
linguiça
lovage
macerate
madeleine
mandoline
mezzaluna
mezze
mole
mouthfeel
nacho
nopal

nuoc mam
orzo
pawpaw
pho
piccata
pierogi
polenta
ponzu
poutine
purslane
quahog
ramekin
rissole
rouille
roux
salsa
sancocho
shawarma
soba
souvlaki
speck
tagine
tamale
tatsoi
teff
tomalley
umami
vindaloo
wasabi
waterzooi
xanthan gum
yakitori
yuca
zabaglione